Great Country Walks Around Toronto

within reach by public transit

Elliott Katz

D0685511

Illustrated by Leong Leung

Great North Books

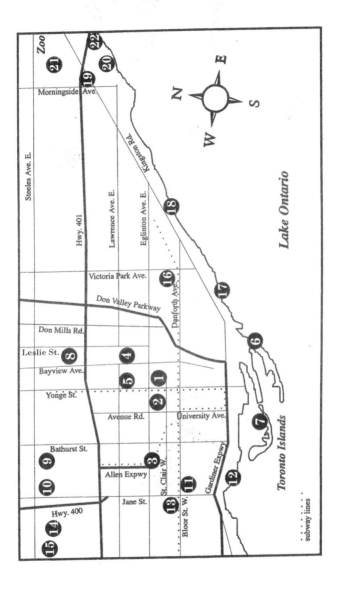

Zoo

21

22

20

19

Morningside Ave.

Kingston Rd.

N
E
W
S

Steeles Ave. E.

Hwy. 401

Lawrence Ave. E.

Eglinton Ave. E.

18

Lake Ontario

Victoria Park Ave.

16

Don Valley Parkway

17

Don Mills Rd.

Danforth Ave.

Leslie St.

8

4

6

Bayview Ave.

5

1

Yonge St.

2

7

Avenue Rd.

University Ave.

Bathurst St.

Toronto Islands

9

3

10

Allen Expwy

St. Clair W.

11

Gardiner Expwy

12

Jane St.

13

Bloor St. W.

Hwy. 400

14

15

········ subway lines

Contents

Trails in the city   **5**

Central
1. Rosedale   **7**
2. Belt Line   **11**
3. Cedarvale Ravine   **15**
4. Wilket Creek – E.T. Seton Park   **19**
5. Sherwood Park   **25**
6. Tommy Thompson Park   **29**
7. Toronto Islands   **32**

North
8. East Don River   **37**
9. West Don River – G. Ross Lord Park   **41**
10. Black Creek   **45**

West
11. High Park   **49**
12. Sunnyside Beaches   **53**
13. Humber River Valley   **57**
14. Humber River and West Humber River   **61**
15. Humber Arboretum   **65**

East
16. Taylor Creek   **69**
17. The Beaches   **73**
18. Scarborough Bluffs   **77**
19. Highland Creek   **81**
20. Lower Highland Creek and East Point Park   **84**
21. Rouge River   **88**
22. Rouge Beach   **93**

ISBN 0-920361-05-6
Revised edition 2006
Sixth edition

Illustration and design: Leong Leung

Printed in Canada
12th printing

Published by:
Great North Books
Toronto, Ontario

Submit comments and updates to:
greatnorthbooks@aol.com

Trade distribution by:
Firefly Books Ltd.
66 Leek Crescent
Richmond Hill, Ontario L4B 1H1
www.fireflybooks.com

**Users of this guide bear full
responsibility for their own safety**
Exercise caution on these paths and streets as you would on
similar paths and streets. Consider the weather, time of day
and other factors. Avoid rivers and streams when there is a
risk of flooding. This guide is not intended for children.

Trails in the city

Walk a forest trail beside a flowing creek, along grassy river banks, through ravines and along wild shores washed by the waves of Lake Ontario. You can see birds, animals, bursting wildflowers in spring and the colors of the leaves in autumn.

Within easy reach of everyone living in or visiting Toronto, but unknown to many, are scenic country trails for walking, exploring, picnics and birdwatching. These paths refresh us with needed contact with nature, away from the stress of city living. Virtually minutes away from a subway station or bus stop, you can be immersed in these natural worlds.

How to reach Toronto's best country walks by TTC public transit or by automobile, exploring the route, and how to get back to the subway or your car from the walk's end are fully detailed here.

Using this book

Each country walk is accompanied by a map for you to follow using the detailed directions in the text. Not all the streets are included on the map, just those needed to help you find your way. To check current TTC schedules go to www.ttc.ca or telephone (416) 393-4636.

Don't let this book sit on your shelf. Put on comfortable walking shoes, pack a snack and go!

1. Rosedale

5 km

Every day thousands of people work or shop on Yonge Street near these nature trails unaware of the diverse wildlife, forests, spring wildflowers and flowing brooks that are so close – great for a relaxing stroll.

Located within minutes from Yonge Street and St. Clair Avenue, the wooded Rosedale ravine offers an escape to nature a few minutes from the center of Toronto.

PUBLIC TRANSIT: From the St. Clair subway station (on the Yonge Street line), walk north on Yonge Street. Turn right on Heath Street East and walk to the end of the street. Here is a sign reading "Nature Trail," and the start of the walk.

AUTOMOBILE: Drive to the corner of Yonge Street and Heath Street East, just north of St. Clair Avenue. Go east on Heath Street East to the end of the street to a sign reading "Nature Trail." Parking in this area can be difficult, and it may be better to take public transit.

THE WALK: Follow the arrow of the "Nature Trail" sign and descend the steps into the ravine. At the bottom turn right and follow the path along the brook, called Yellow Creek. Pass under the St. Clair Avenue bridge, and after crossing a footbridge, enter David Balfour Park. Going south through Balfour Park you pass under the Summerhill railroad bridge and soon reach busy Mount Pleasant Road. Carefully cross Mount

Pleasant Road – there is no traffic light – and follow the path indicated by the "Park Drive Reservation" sign.

You soon reach a trail junction. If you want to end the walk, take the path leading to Creighleigh Gardens and take Milkman's Road to South Drive. From there, you can take the Rosedale 82 bus to Rosedale subway station (on the Yonge Street line), or the Sherbourne 75 bus to the Sherbourne station (on the Bloor-Danforth line).

To continue this walk, go left at this junction and follow the sign to Moore Park Ravine. The path enters the Don Valley and skirts a Bayview Avenue ramp. You also pass the old Don Valley Brick Works, founded in 1882. Bricks made here were used in building the Ontario Legislature and Casa Loma. Here you can see the quarry, an old industrial building and geological features.

Follow the path north along a ridge through the maples and willows of Moore Park ravine and gradually ascend to Moore Avenue. Cross Moore Avenue.

From here, you can take the South Leaside 88 bus back to your starting point at the St. Clair subway station.

To continue the walk, enter the Mount Pleasant Cemetery, which is open from dawn to dusk, and follow the Belt Line Trail signs through the cemetery's eastern section, under Mount Pleasant Avenue and through the cemetery's western half.

Take the stairs that lead down to Yonge Street. Go right on Yonge Street and walk to the

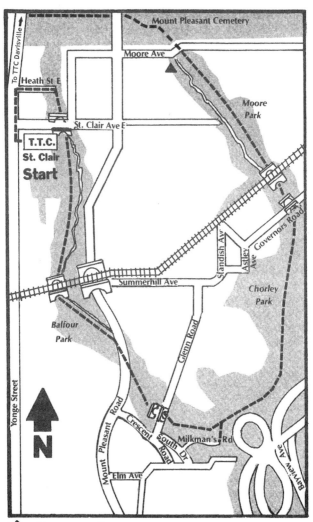

To TTC Davisville

Heath St E

St. Clair Ave E

T.T.C.
St. Clair
Start

Moore Ave

Mount Pleasant Cemetery

Moore Park

Governors Road

Standish Av

Astley Ave

Chorley Park

Summerhill Ave

Balfour Park

Yonge Street

Glenn Road

Mount Pleasant Road

Crescent Road

South Dr

Milkman's Rd

Elm Ave

Bayview Ave

N

⌂ - Washrooms   ▲ - Water Fountain

Davisville subway station (on the Yonge Street line) at the corner of Yonge Street and Davisville Road.

Instead of going down the stairs, you can stay on the Belt Line Trail and go across the footbridge – an old railway bridge – over Yonge Street and continue on the Belt Line Trail described separately in this guide.

GETTING BACK: At Davisville subway station you're one stop north of the starting point at St. Clair subway station.

Saving the Rosedale Ravine

Toronto is fortunate to have wooded ravines accessible to everyone. It was not always so. In February 1955, a local resident learned that a developer had bought land on the ravine's edge and planned to construct an apartment building that would descend 38 meters into the idyllic wooded ravine. The building would have three storeys on the table-land and nine storeys anchored to the ravine wall. The law then in force limited the height of buildings on the table-land, but did not deal with descent into the ravine.

A "Save the Ravines" group was formed. They campaigned for city government to stop the construction plans. On February 21, 1955, crews began cutting trees in the ravine. On February 28, Mayor Nathan Phillips and the Board of Controllers voted to not allow the construction. The City Council also voted to expropriate the Rosedale ravine to preserve its natural character.

2. Belt Line Trail

4 km

The Belt Line Trail is an old railway right-of-way that is now a picturesque tree-lined path through Forest Hill. During the 1880s, Toronto was experiencing a real estate boom. Real estate developer John Moore built the Belt Line Railway to encourage people to buy homes in the then-new suburbs of Moore Park and upper Forest Hill near Bathurst Street and Eglinton Avenue West. He promoted the railway as a fast way to commute to the city.

Service began in 1892 with six trains per day in each direction. Two years later, passenger service was discontinued due to insufficient traffic. Too few people had moved to these suburbs to support the service. Today the rails are gone and the Belt Line is a linear park.

PUBLIC TRANSIT: From Davisville subway station (on the Yonge Street line), go right on Chaplin Crescent. Turn left on Lascelles Boulevard. Walk through Oriole Park to Frobisher Avenue and the Belt Line Trail.

AUTOMOBILE: Go to Yonge Street and Chaplin Cresent. Park in the area. From Yonge Street, go right on Chaplin Crescent and turn left on Lascelles Boulevard to Oriole Park. Walk through Oriole Park to Frobisher Avenue and the Belt Line Trail.

THE WALK: Follow the Belt Line Trail through Forest Hill. When you reach Oriole Parkway and Avenue Road, cross these streets at the nearest traffic lights. Continue on the trail and go under the Eglinton Avenue West bridge. Cross Bathurst Street at the nearest traffic lights.

Follow the path all the way to the Allen Expressway. Turn left and walk on the sidewalk along the Allen Expressway to Eglinton Avenue West. Go right on Eglinton Avenue to the Eglinton West subway station (on the Spadina line). The Cedarvale Ravine walk, described separately, begins here.

GETTING BACK: From here you can take the subway at Eglinton West station. To return to the starting point at Davisville subway station (on the Yonge Street line), take the Eglinton West 32 bus east to Eglinton subway station (on the Yonge Street line) and take the subway south for one stop to Davisville station.

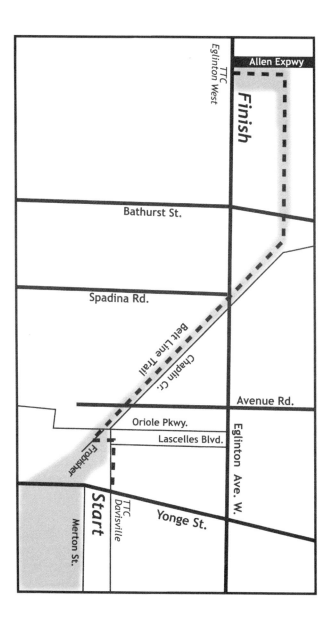

ON THE TORONTO BELT LINE RAILWAY.

FOREST HILL—ON BATHURST STREET.

The Belt Line near Bathurst Street and Eglinton Avenue West as depicted in Moore's real estate brochure.

3. Cedarvale Ravine

2.5 km

Over 30 species of birds nest in the wooded Cedarvale ravine. During the spring and fall, migrating birds can be seen here. Among the species that can be observed are Cardinals, Great Horned Owls, Barred Owls, and several species of finches. In winter, birds are attracted by the feeding stations in the nearby gardens.

Flowing through the Cedarvale ravine is Castle Frank Brook, named after the summer residence of Lieutenant Governor John Simcoe and his wife Elizabeth. In her diary, Elizabeth Simcoe wrote: "We found the river very shallow in many parts and obstructed by trees. A bald eagle sat on a blasted pine on a very bald point."

In the late 1960s and early 1970s the Cedarvale ravine was part of the proposed route of the Spadina Expressway. In June 1971, after protests by citizens' groups, the government halted construction of the expressway (now called the W.R.Allen Expressway) at Eglinton Avenue West and prevented the destruction of this ravine.

PUBLIC TRANSIT: Go to Eglinton West subway station (on the Spadina line), and exit onto Eglinton Avenue West. Walk to the right and cross Eglinton Avenue at the traffic lights and then go to the left along Eglinton Avenue. Turn right on Everden Road and walk down this street to Ava Road. Here is the path leading through Cedarvale Park to the Cedarvale ravine.

AUTOMOBILE: Park your car on a street near Eglinton West subway station, which is located on Eglinton Avenue West, west of Bathurst Street. Opposite the Eglinton West subway station, walk down Everden Road to Ava Road and the Cedarvale path.

THE WALK: Follow the path through Cedarvale Park to the wide and deep Cedarvale ravine. The path through the ravine follows Castle Frank Brook and goes under the Glen Cedar Road bridge and the Bathurst Street bridge. The path eventually ascends to Heath Street West and an entrance to the St. Clair West subway station (on the Spadina line), one stop south of this walk's starting point at Eglinton West subway station.

Elizabeth Simcoe and her diary

As someone who loved to walk in the outdoors, Elizabeth Simcoe explored and gave names to many of the natural areas described in this book. In 1791, at age 25, she left Wolford, her estate in

John Graves Simcoe   *Elizabeth Simcoe*

J.R. Robertson Collection, Toronto Library

Start

T.T.C. | Eglinton West

Everden Rd.

Ava Rd.

Bathurst St.

Strateam Rd.

Glen Cedar Rd.

Cedarvale Park

N

Spadina Rd.

Cedarvale ravine

Vaughan Rd.

St. Clair West

T.T.C.

Montclair Ave.

Finish

 = Washrooms   = Water Fountain

Devonshire, England, and came here with her husband John Graves Simcoe who had been appointed Lieutenant-Governor of Upper Canada – which, later became the province of Ontario.

Elizabeth Simcoe faced life in the Canadian wilderness with enthusiasm. She traveled extensively in the Toronto (then called York), Niagara, Queenston and Gananoque areas and recorded her impressions in her diary. The daily entries and her sketches vividly depict the land and life in Ontario's early pioneering days. Her drawings are among the earliest pictorial records available of the area. In 1796, the Simcoes returned to England and their Wolford estate.

4. Wilket Creek – E.T. Seton Park

5 km

The valleys of Wilket Creek and the West Don River, are part of one of the largest natural areas in Toronto. A great variety of birds can be seen on this scenic walk. It is especially beautiful in the spring when migrating birds are here among the bursting spring wildflowers. The starting point at Edwards Gardens, which was part of the estate of wealthy paint manufacturer Rupert Edwards, is landscaped with floral displays and rock gardens. The slopes of the ravine are covered with colorful flowers, plants, shrubs and trees. The rock gardens contain 426 tons of Credit Valley stone.

Wilket Creek is a narrow wooded park where abundant birdlife can be seen. Its natural state contrasts with the manicured Edwards Gardens. The West Don River flows through the wide open valley of E.T. Seton Park, named after the world-famous artist-naturalist and author whose love of nature was inspired here in the 1870s.

This walk can be combined with the Taylor Creek walk for a total of 10 km ending at the Victoria Park subway station (on the Bloor-Danforth line).

PUBLIC TRANSIT: From the Eglinton subway station (on the Yonge Street line), take the Lawrence East 54 bus to Edwards Gardens at

Leslie Street and Lawrence Avenue East.

AUTOMOBILE: Edwards Gardens is located on Lawrence Avenue East, just west of the intersection of Leslie Street. The entrance to the parking lot is on Leslie Street just south of Lawrence Avenue.

THE WALK: After enjoying the floral displays of Edwards Gardens, take a path down into the ravine. When you reach the creek, go left towards the sign for Wilket Creek Park. Soon after entering Wilket Creek Park, you come to a sign indicating that it's 1.5 km to Eglinton Avenue East.

When you reach the park road leading to Eglinton Avenue East, you can end the walk here by walking out to the street and taking one of the buses going west on Eglinton Avenue to Eglinton subway station (on the Yonge Street line).

To continue the walk, turn left on the park road and go under the Eglinton Avenue East bridge. Cross the footbridge over the creek and continue south into E.T. Seton Park. Pass under the railway bridge. You soon reach a side path leading up to Don Mills Road, from where you can take the Don Mills 25 bus to Pape subway station (on the Bloor-Danforth line).

Continuing south through E.T. Seton Park, you pass under the Overlea Boulevard bridge and eventually reach a sign reading "Edwards Gardens 5 km, Sunnybrook Park 5 km." From here, you can retrace your route back to Edwards Gardens. If you want to continue on the Taylor Creek walk, go to the left here and follow that walk. To get back by TTC, go right and follow the

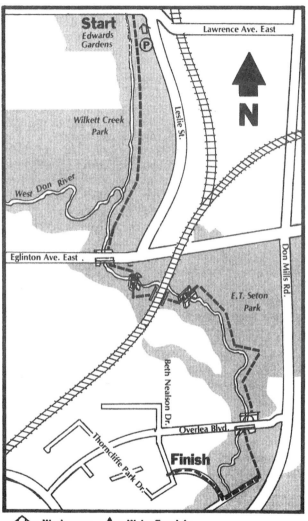

Start
Edwards
Gardens

Lawrence Ave. East

Leslie St.

Wilkett Creek
Park

West Don River

Eglinton Ave. East .

Don Mills Rd.

E.T. Seton
Park

Beth Nealson Dr.

Thorncliffe Park Dr.

Overlea Blvd.

Finish

N

⬆ = Washrooms   🔺 = Water Fountain

road parallel to the railway tracks. Then turn right up the hill leading to Thorncliffe Park Drive.

GETTING BACK: To your right on Thorncliffe Park Drive is the stop for the Thorncliffe Park 81 bus, which goes to Pape subway station (on the Bloor-Danforth line). The bus stops on this side of the street after 3:30 p.m. Before 3:30 p.m. it circles Thorncliffe Park Drive on the other side of the street.

On weekdays and Saturdays you can take the South Leaside 88 bus from either side of Thorncliffe Park Drive (take the bus that comes first) to St. Clair subway station (on the Yonge Street line).

To get back to Edwards Gardens, walk out to, but don't cross Overlea Boulevard, and take the Don Mills 25 bus east along Overlea Boulevard and north on Don-Mills Road to Lawrence Avenue East. Then take the Lawrence East 54 bus west to Leslie Street.

Ernest Thompson Seton

Artist-naturalist and author Ernest Thompson Seton explored the wilderness of the Don River Valley in the 1870s. His stories based on his experiences and observations here became famous world-wide bestsellers. Born in 1860 in South Shields, Durham, England, E.T. Seton immigrated with his family to Canada in 1866, settling in Toronto in 1870.

Ernest built a small cabin in the woods near the Don River where he retreated after school and

Toronto Reference Library

E.T. Seton

23

on weekends to collect shells and feathers and live a Robinson Crusoe-type life. "To a small boy, as I was then, it was a wild and distant country. To me, it was paradise," he later wrote.

He enrolled in the Ontario College of Art and at age 19 won the college's Gold Medal. He then went to study in England, where he spent many days at the natural history collection of the British Museum, visiting the London Zoo and starving due to lack of money.

Back in Canada, Seton began writing simple but moving stories about the adventures and personalities of animals he watched in the Don Valley. Silverspot was a wise old crow who taught the other crows in the valley the tricks of keeping safe from armed men and horned owls. Seton observed a mother partridge, pretending to be injured, flapping along the ground just out of reach of Reynard the fox, distracting him from her little chick Redruff.

In 1898 these two stories plus six others were published in *Wild Animals I Have Known*, the first of Seton's 40 books. It was a bestseller and has been published in 15 foreign editions.

Rudyard Kipling's Jungle Books were inspired by Seton's stories, and American President and naturalist Theodore Roosevelt was one of Seton's greatest admirers.

Seton later moved to the United States and was chief of the Boy Scouts of America from 1910 to 1915. He died on October 23, 1946 at the age of 86 at his ranch in New Mexico.

5. Sherwood Park

5.5 km

Starting at the floral displays of the Alexander Muir Gardens, this walk goes through thick forests of white pine, beech and oak in one of the largest natural areas in Toronto. At pastoral Sunnybrook Park, the route turns north through the forests along the West Don River and emerges at the Glendon College campus of York University. The West Don River is a major tributary of the Don River, named by Lieutenant Governor John Graves Simcoe after the Don River in central England.

PUBLIC TRANSIT: From Lawrence subway station (on the Yonge Street line), exit to the northeast corner of the intersection of Lawrence Avenue and Yonge Street. Cross Lawrence Avenue and continue south on Yonge Street to St. Edmunds Drive and the Alexander Muir Memorial Gardens.

AUTOMOBILE: Park your car on a side street near Yonge Street and Lawrence Avenue. Walk south on Yonge Street to St. Edmunds Drive and the Alexander Muir Memorial Gardens.

THE WALK: Enter Alexander Muir Gardens, named for the composer of "The Maple Leaf Forever" a patriotic song about Canada. Go down the steps and walk through the gardens. Follow the path to the road. Go left, walk to the end of the road and take the path into the ravine.

The path goes under the Mount Pleasant Road bridge and eventually ascends at Blythwood Road. Cross Blythwood Road to the "Nature Trail" sign and descend into the ravine. After passing a children's playground, another "Nature Trail" sign indicates the trail turns left. Climb the steps up the hillside. The path eventually emerges at Bayview Avenue.

Go left on Bayview Avenue. Cross Bayview Avenue at the traffic lights at Blythwood Road and enter the grounds of Sunnybrook Hospital. At the first stop sign, go right at the Toronto Sunnybrook Regional Cancer Centre. Then turn left and walk on the sidewalk. Just past the Sunnybrook Centre for Independent Living, follow the road as it curves around to the left. Go right on the road marked "Dead End, No Exit." Take this road down through a wooded area to a bridge over the West Don River.

From here, if you want to reach Wilket Creek and E.T. Seton Park: cross the bridge, turn right at the sign indicating "Eglinton Avenue and TTC" and follow the park road.

To continue this walk, don't cross the bridge, and go to your left and take the path into Glendon Forest. Follow the path along the river. You eventually reach the playing fields at Glendon College. Walk to the end of the field and go left along the road.

GETTING BACK: Go through Glendon College to Bayview Avenue. Cross Lawrence Avenue and take the Sunnybrook 124 (which runs daily) or the Lawrence-Donway 162 (no service on Saturdays or Sundays) west to the Lawrence subway station (on the Yonge Street line) this walk's start. You can also take the Bayview 11 south to Davisville subway station (on the Yonge Street line).

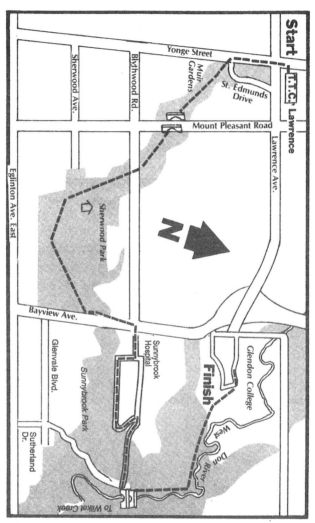

⌂ = Washrooms ▲ = Water Fountain

6. Tommy Thompson Park

10 km return

Lagoons, beaches and wildflowers are found in Tommy Thompson Park, a 5-km peninsula also known as the Leslie Street Spit, which juts into Lake Ontario from south of Leslie Street and extends beyond the eastern end of the Toronto Islands. A cool breeze blows in off the lake during the summer.

The lagoons on the headland are home or stopover for migrating sandpipers and the largest colony of ring-billed seagulls in the world. The spit has also attracted a breeding colony of terns, as well as other species of geese, seagulls and ducks.

The headland was named after Tommy Thompson, Toronto's popular first Parks Commissioner. Thompson was well known for his "Please Walk on the Grass" signs and the walks he led in Toronto's natural areas.

Tommy Thompson Park is operated by the Toronto and Region Conservation Authority which offers interpretive programs on weekends and holidays during the summer including nature walks on bird life, mammals, reptiles and butterflies. Pets are not permitted at the park. A free shuttle van operates in the park from early May to mid-October. You can board the van at the main gate, the pedestrian bridge or along the route.

For information: www.trca.on.ca telephone (416) 661-6600, email: **info@trca.on.ca**

HOURS: Tommy Thompson Park is open year-round on weekends and holidays except December 25 and 26 and January 1. Hours are from 9 a.m. to 6 p.m. from April to October and 9 a.m. to 4:30 from November to March.

PUBLIC TRANSIT: Take the Queen Street streetcar from Queen subway station (on the Yonge Street line) or Osgoode subway station (on the University line) to Leslie Street and walk south on Leslie Street.

From Donlands subway station (on the Bloor-Danforth line) you can take the Jones 83 bus (it doesn't run on Sundays) south to Leslie Street and Commissioners Street, and then walk south on Leslie Street.

AUTOMOBILE: Drive along Lake Shore Boulevard East and turn south down Leslie Street toward the lake. There is parking along Leslie Street and Unwin Avenue.

THE WALK: After passing through the gate at the corner of Leslie Street and Unwin Avenue, walk south and connect with the roadway along the headland. After about 1.5 km there is a path on your right which leads to a sand beach.

The main route continues to the end of the headland where the path climbs to the Toronto Harbour Lighthouse. From this vantage point you have a tremendous view of the lagoons and on a clear day you can see the shores of the United States, 50 km away.

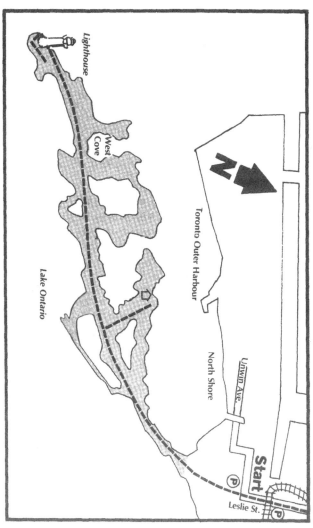

Lighthouse

West Cove

Toronto Outer Harbour

Lake Ontario

North Shore

Unwin Ave.

Start

Leslie St.

 = Washrooms   = Water Fountain

7. Toronto Islands

Ward's Island to Hanlan's Point 5.25 km
Ward's Island to Centre Island 3.25 km
Centre Island to Hanlan's Point 2 km

Eight minutes away by ferry boat from downtown are the enchanting Toronto Islands, a chain of islands separated by channels and small bays. Within its 365 hectares of parkland are sandy beaches, sand dunes and forests. There is also fishing, canoeing and sailing here.

"The water in the bay is beautifully clear and transparent. The air on these sands is peculiarly clear and fine. The Indians esteem this place so healthy that they come and stay here when they are ill," wrote Elizabeth Simcoe about this area. Her husband, Lieutenant-Governor John Simcoe chose Toronto as the provincial capital because he believed he could fortify the site and defend it from an American invasion. An important factor in the defense of Toronto were the military advantages offered by the Toronto Islands in guarding the city. Historical markers indicate the location of the military positions on the island.

The Toronto Islands were once a peninsula attached to Toronto but during a storm in 1858 the waters of Lake Ontario broke through part of the peninsula and the islands were created. Among the abundant birdlife that can be seen are Canada geese, mallards, grackles, wrens, owls, ruby-throated hummingbirds, Black-crowned Night herons and snow geese. In late summer and fall, migrating shorebirds and one of the largest concentrations of Saw-whet owls in the world can been seen here.

PUBLIC TRANSIT: Take either of the north-south subway lines to Union station. From here, you can walk on Bay Street to Queens Quay West, or transfer to the Harbourfront 509 or the Spadina 510 street car and get off at Queens Quay station. The ferry terminal is on Queens Quay West at the foot of Bay Street just beside the Harbour Castle Westin Hotel.

AUTOMOBILE: There are parking lots along Queen's Quay near the ferry docks which are at the foot of Bay Street. During the summer, finding a parking space may be difficult and you may want to leave your car at home or near a subway station and take the subway.

FERRIES: Ferry service is operated to Ward's Island, Centre Island and Hanlan's Point. For schedules and fares: **www.toronto.ca/parks/island/** or call (416) 392-8193.

THE WALK: All the pathways on the Toronto Islands offer pleasant and relaxing country walking. Signs here read: "Please walk on the grass." The most scenic and wild walk is along the shore of Lake Ontario from Ward's Island to Hanlan's Point. You can take the ferry to any of the three points and walk to the lakeshore. The description here begins at Ward's Island.

From the Ward's Island ferry dock, follow the sign, "To Boardwalk and Beach," and walk to the boardwalk. Go to the right and walk along the boardwalk and enjoy the view of the Outer

Harbour Headland and Lake Ontario. In winter huge waves crash over the breakwater.

At Centre Island is a concrete pier extending into the lake. Opposite the pier is the path across Centre Island to the Centre Island ferry dock.

Continue along the lakeshore to the Gibraltar Lighthouse, which was built in 1808. It is believed to be haunted by its first keeper who disappeared mysteriously in 1815. Part of a human skeleton was later found nearby.

Past the lighthouse is a pond. Beyond the pond, take the path onto the sand dunes on the lakeshore. These driftwood-strewn beaches are the wildest section of the walk. Hike all the way to the fence at the end of the beach and then walk to the right to Hanlan's Point, named for the family of world-champion sculler Ned Hanlan who lived here and was elected alderman in 1898. The area was originally known as Gibraltar Point as it guarded the entrance to the harbor of Toronto. By 1800 there were two storehouses and a guard house here which were destroyed by the Americans during their second raid on the city in 1813 during the War of 1812-14.

Walk to the Hanlan's Point ferry dock. From here take the ferry back to the mainland, or walk back to the Centre Island ferry or to the Ward's Island ferry.

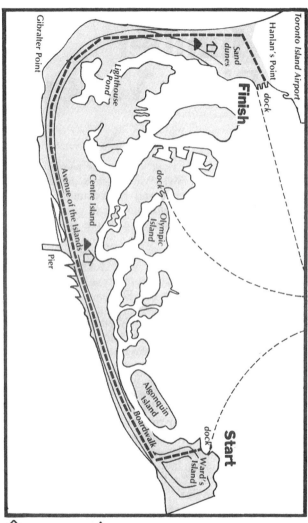

Toronto Island Airport

Hanlan's Point

Gibralter Point

Sand dunes

Finish

Lighthouse Pond

dock

Olympic Island

dock

Centre Island

Avenue of the Islands

Pier

Algonquin Island

Boardwalk

dock

Start

Ward's Island

⌂ = **Washrooms**   ▲ = **Water Fountain**

"It is good to collect things;
it is better to take walks."

— Anatole France

8. East Don River

6 km

When Governor John Simcoe and his wife Elizabeth arrived in Toronto in 1791, the Don River Valley was a wilderness of mixed forests inhabited by deer, wolves and other wildlife. In her diary, Elizabeth Simcoe wrote that on a wintry day in January 1794, she went to the Don River and saw the tracks of wolves in the snow.

For centuries people have traveled the Don River Valley. At the time of the Simcoes, the Don was used for canoeing in summer and sledding in winter. In the 19th century, railways were built along the southern part of the Don River. In the 20th century the Don Valley Parkway was built here.

This path, near Toronto's northern boundary, explores a wooded area along the East Don River away from railways and highways.

PUBLIC TRANSIT: From Leslie subway station (on the Sheppard line), exit to the southwest corner of Sheppard Avenue East and Leslie Street. Cross Sheppard Avenue East. On the northwest corner of Sheppard Avenue East and Leslie Street is a concrete wall that reads "Don River Trail." Go down the path to the main trail.

It is also possible to take GO Transit to Oriole station, and walk north on Leslie Street to Sheppard Avenue East. For information on GO schedules, go to **www.gotransit.ca** telephone 416-869-3200 or toll-free 1-888 GET ON GO (438-6646).

AUTOMOBILE: If you're going westbound on Sheppard Avenue: just west of Leslie Street turn right where the sign indicates "To Old Leslie St." Then turn right into the first driveway. It leads down to a parking lot. On your left as you enter the parking lot is the trail.

If you're going eastbound on Sheppard Avenue: west of Leslie Street turn right onto Old Leslie Street. At the top of the hill, go right and cross the bridge over Sheppard Avenue. After crossing the bridge, turn right. Just before Sheppard Avenue, turn left into a driveway. It leads to a parking lot. The trail is on your left as you reach the parking lot.

THE WALK: Follow the path through the forest. When you reach tennis courts, go left on the path. Continue on the path and go under the Finch Avenue East bridge. Stay on the trail and go under the Cummer Avenue bridge. Continue on the main trail and you eventually reach Leslie Street just south of Steeles Avenue East.

GETTING BACK: From here you can walk back to the starting point, or take the Leslie 51 bus (it doesn't operate on Sundays) south to the Leslie subway station (on the Sheppard line). You can also walk north on Leslie Street, cross Steeles Avenue East and take the Steeles East 53 to Finch subway station (on the Yonge Street line).

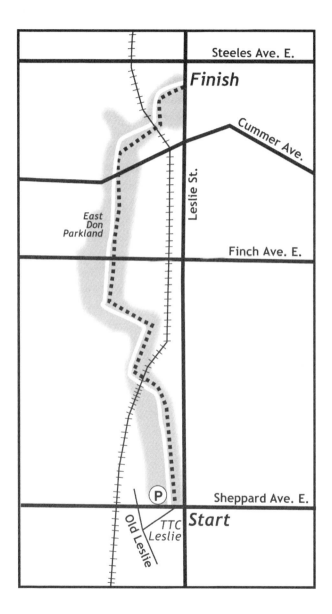

Steeles Ave. E.

Finish

Cummer Ave.

Leslie St.

East
Don
Parkland

Finch Ave. E.

Sheppard Ave. E.

(P)

TTC
Leslie

Old Leslie

Start

*"In every walk with nature, one receives far more
than one seeks."*

— *John Muir*

9. West Don River – G. Ross Lord Park

3 km

One of the three branches of the Don River, the West Don River begins in the hills of the Oak Ridges Moraine between Maple and Richmond Hill and flows south entering Toronto in wooded G. Ross Lord Park near the city's northern boundary. In this park are wetland areas where a variety of wildlife can be seen. After leaving the park, the West Don River flows east and meets the East Don River and Taylor Creek at the Forks of the Don near the Don Valley Parkway.

This park was named after Dr. G. Ross Lord, who led the Metropolitan Toronto and Region Conservation Authority from 1958 to 1972. The Don River's only dam, the G. Ross Lord dam on the park's south side was built in 1973 to protect the area south of the park from flooding.

PUBLIC TRANSIT: From Finch subway station (on the Yonge Street line), take the Steeles West 60 bus to Steeles Avenue West and Thurman Road which is on the north side of Steeles Avenue. On the south side of Steeles Avenue is Torresdale Avenue. Cross Steeles Avenue at the traffic light and walk down Torresdale Avenue. Go right on Fisherville Road and walk to the park entrance. The address on the park sign is 175 Fisherville Road.

AUTOMOBILE: From Bathurst Street and Fisherville Road, which is one street south of Steeles Avenue West, go west on Fisherville Road to the park entrance at 175 Fisherville Road. There is parking on the street near the park entrance.

THE WALK: From the park entrance on Fisherville Road, walk along the path. When you reach a children's playground, go right and follow the path as it crosses the West Don River. When you come to a junction where the path on the left goes up a hill (this leads to the park entrance on Dufferin Street), go right and walk along the path. You cross the West Don River several times. The path leads to Steeles Avenue West.

GETTING BACK: From the end of the trail, you can retrace your steps to your starting point, or you can go right on Steeles Avenue West and walk to nearest TTC bus stop and take the Steeles West 60 bus to Finch subway station (on the Yonge Street line).

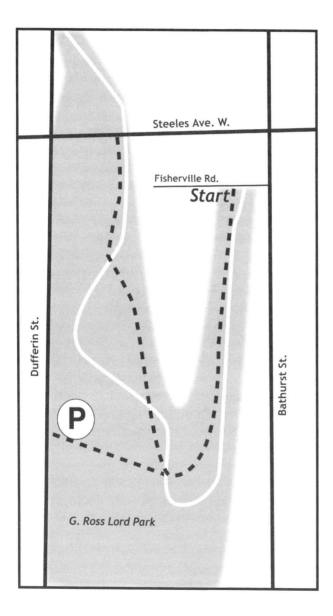

Steeles Ave. W.

Fisherville Rd.

Start

Dufferin St.

Bathurst St.

P

G. Ross Lord Park

*"Before supper walk a little, after supper
do the same."*

— *Erasmus*

10. Black Creek

5 km

A tributary of the Humber River, Black Creek flows through a wooded valley where birds and other wildlife can be seen. Situated near Toronto's northern boundary, this walk is just west of the York University campus.

When a flash rainstorm hit Toronto on August 19, 2005, severe flooding occurred at Black Creek. More than 140 millimeters of rain fell in a three hour period in this area – compared to 210 millimeters in 12 hours during Hurricane Hazel in October 1954. Parts of the city were submerged. As the surrounding roads don't absorb water, the heavy rainfall flowed to valleys and ravines and flooded them. Black Creek became a powerful torrent that washed away 30 meters of the road surface of Finch Avenue West including the Finch Avenue bridge over the creek, leaving a deep canyon. After the flood waters subsided the damage was repaired.

PUBLIC TRANSIT: From Jane subway station (on the Bloor-Danforth line) take the Jane 35B to Black Creek Pioneer Village on Murray Ross Parkway between Shoreham Drive and Steeles Avenue West.

Or, from Finch subway station (on the Yonge Street line), take the Steeles West 60 bus to Murray Ross Parkway. Walk down Murray Ross Parkway to Black Creek Pioneer Village.

AUTOMOBILE: From Steeles Avenue West, go south on Murray Ross Parkway, located east of

Jane Street. Turn right to Black Creek Pioneer Village and go into the parking lot. There is a fee for parking.

THE WALK: Near the southern end of the Black Creek Pioneer Village parking lot is the path leading down to the trail along Black Creek. Take this trail down to the valley, go left and walk south along Black Creek. You soon reach Finch Avenue West. The address on the Black Creek Parklands sign here reads 1650 Finch Avenue West. If you want to end the walk here, you can cross Finch Avenue at the traffic lights at Sentinel Road to the left and take the Finch West 36 bus to Finch station (on the Yonge Street line).

To continue the walk, cross Finch Avenue to the left at the traffic lights at Sentinel Road and go south into Derrydowns Park which has picnic tables and washrooms. Walk until you reach Sheppard Avenue West. Cross Sheppard Avenue at the traffic light to the right at Arleta Avenue and Northover Street. Continue into Downsview Dells Park. The address on the park sign here reads 1651 Sheppard Avenue West. Here are barbecues, picnic tables and washrooms. Walk along the park road through a wide open picturesque valley. After exploring this park, walk back to Sheppard Avenue West.

GETTING BACK: You can retrace your route along the trail to the Black Creek Pioneer Village parking lot. Or, from the entrance to Downsview Dells Park on Sheppard Avenue West, take the Sheppard West 84 bus to Downsview subway station (on the Spadina line) or to Sheppard-Yonge subway station.

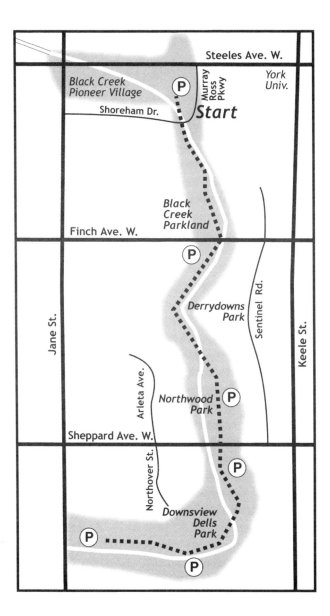

Steeles Ave. W.

York Univ.

P Murray Ross Pkwy

Black Creek Pioneer Village

Shoreham Dr.

Start

Black Creek Parkland

Finch Ave. W.

P

Derrydowns Park

Sentinel Rd.

Jane St.

Keele St.

Arleta Ave.

Northwood Park

P

Sheppard Ave. W.

Northover St.

P

Downsview Dells Park

P

P

11. High Park

5 km

High Park is 137 hectares of hills, forests, streams. Many species of waterfowl can be seen on High Park's Grenadier Pond, especially during the spring and autumn when migrating ducks, seagulls, geese, grebes and swallows visit the park. You can also rent rowboats at the pond.

High Park was a gift to Toronto by John Howard, an architect who came to Toronto in 1832 and was made city surveyor by Toronto's first mayor William Lyon Mackenzie. In 1836 Howard bought 67 hectares here and built his home which he called Colborne Lodge after Sir John Colborne, then Lieutenant Governor of Ontario. Howard donated the property as a public park in 1873.

Over the years, additional land was added to the park. Colborne Lodge is now a museum containing original furnishings including the kitchen and fireplace, and early Canadian art.

PUBLIC TRANSIT: Go to High Park subway station (on the Bloor-Danforth line) and exit onto High Park Avenue. Go to the right, down High Park Avenue and cross Bloor Street West to the entrance of High Park.

AUTOMOBILE: From Bloor Street West, turn south into High Park through the entrance opposite High Park Avenue. Take the West Road and park in one of the designated lots. From May to October, cars are restricted from certain parts of the park and it may be necessary to park along Bloor Street or High Park Avenue.

THE WALK: From the entrance to High Park, walk west along Bloor Street on the edge of the park to a sign reading "Nature Trail." Follow the arrow and walk on the path along the side of the ravine. Here the trees have signs indicating their species.

The trail gradually descends to the shore of Grenadier Pond, named for the British soldiers who used to do their drills on the frozen lake during winters in the mid-19th century.

At the southern end of the pond, turn left and go along the path. The trail leads to The Queensway. If you want to end the walk here, you can cross The Queensway and get on the Queen Street 501 streetcar which goes to Osgoode subway station (on the University line) and Queen subway station (on the Yonge Street line), or the Lakeshore 508 streetcar to St. Andrew subway station (on the University line) and King subway station (on the Yonge Street line).

To continue the walk, stay on the path, cross Colborne Lodge Drive and follow the path as it turns left back into High Park. The walk crosses Deer Pen Road. Follow the trail uphill as it parallels Spring Road and gradually ascends out of the forest. Turn right on Colborne Lodge Drive to the park entrance.

GETTING BACK: Cross Bloor Street West and walk up High Park Avenue to the High Park subway station (on the Bloor-Danforth line).

OTHER ATTRACTIONS: Other facilities in High Park that you might want to visit include: 1.

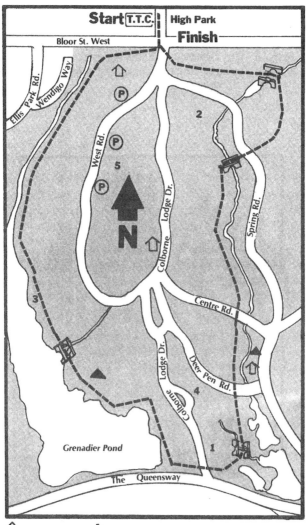

Start **T.T.C.** High Park **Finish**

Bloor St. West

Ellis Park Rd.
Wendigo Way

West Rd.

Colborne Lodge Dr.

Spring Rd.

N

2

5

3

Centre Rd.

Lodge Dr.

Colborne

Deer Pen Rd.

4

1

Grenadier Pond

The Queensway

 = Washrooms   = Water Fountain

Colborne Lodge. 2. Sculpture Symposium Area. 3. The Bandstand, featuring free evening and Sunday afternoon concerts during the summer. 4. High Park Zoo. 5. Swimming Pool.

12. Sunnyside Beaches

4 km

A cool breeze off Lake Ontario makes this a pleasant walk on a hot summer's day through parkland along the shores of Lake Ontario from the mouth of the Humber River west to Ontario Place. The western half of this route is along sandy and grass beaches while the eastern half is a walkway right on the lakeshore.

Along the beach are picnic tables, a swimming pool and a playground for children. Just offshore is a breakwater which is a resting place for ducks and gulls including some uncommon species such as Glaucous Gulls, Iceland Gulls, Herring Gulls and Great Black-backed Gulls. During the spring and fall, migrating terns can also be seen here.

PUBLIC TRANSIT: There are several ways to reach this walk. From Dundas West subway station (on the Bloor-Danforth line) and take the King 504 streetcar down Roncesvalles Avenue to The Queensway. Get off the streetcar here, cross The Queensway to the walkway over the Gardiner Expressway. This brings you to the Palais Royale Ballroom at approximately the mid-point of this walk.

To reach the eastern end of this walk, you can take the Bathurst 511 street car from Bathurst subway station (on the Bloor-Danforth line), or the

Harbourfront 509 street car from Union subway station (at the south end of both north-south subway lines) to the streetcar loop near Exhibition Place. From here, walk west along the Waterfront Trail.

AUTOMOBILE: The Sunnyside Beaches are along Lake Shore Boulevard West. Parking lots are located at the foot of Windermere Avenue and at the foot of Ellis Avenue at the western end of the walk near the mouth of the Humber River.

THE WALK: The western part of this walk, to your right if you came via the walkway from the foot of Roncesvalles Avenue, is grassy parkland with sandy beaches. Walk right along the water and enjoy the beautiful blue colour of Lake Ontario.

Along the way is a monument honoring Sir Casimir Gzowski, an engineer who was co-founder of the company that built the Grand Trunk Railway between Toronto and Sarnia. In the 1870s, he designed and built the International Bridge across the Niagara River. He was also the first chairman of the Niagara Falls Parks Commission and planned the park system along the Canadian side which visitors still enjoy today.

The western end of this walk is near the mouth of the Humber River. The Lion Monument was erected here in August 1940 at the entrance to the Queen Elizabeth Way to commemorate its opening in 1939 by Queen Elizabeth and King George VI on the first trip of the British Sovereign to Canada.

Going east from the walkway at the foot of Roncesvalles Avenue, the path parallels Lake

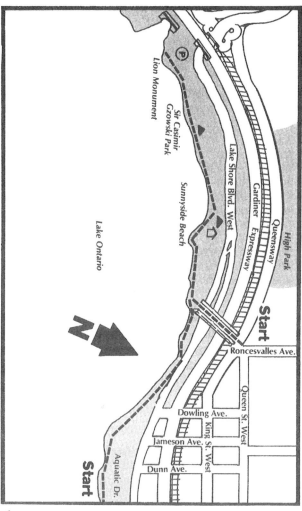

Lion Monument

Sir Casimir Gzowski Park

Sunnyside Beach

Lake Shore Blvd. West

Gardiner Expressway

Queensway

High Park

Lake Ontario

N

Start

Roncesvalles Ave.

Queen St. West

Dowling Ave.

King St. West

Jameson Ave.

Dunn Ave.

Aquatic Dr.

Start

 = Washrooms   = Water Fountain

Shore Boulevard West and goes past the Boulevard Club, the Toronto Sailing and Canoe Club and the Argonaut Rowing Club. Just past here is Aquatic Drive, a walkway right along Lake Ontario's scenic shore. Walk this path to just outside of Ontario Place and Exhibition Place.

GETTING BACK: You can retrace your route. Or, from the street car loop near Exhibition Place, take the Bathurst 511 street car to Bathurst subway station (on the Bloor-Danforth line), or the Harbourfront 509 street car to Union subway station (at the south end of both north-south subway lines).

13. Humber River Valley

6 km

The wooded and steep-walled Humber River Valley is one of Toronto's major river valleys. Ducks swim in the river and shorebirds, seagulls and migrant birds can be seen here in the spring and autumn.

On September 9, 1615, in the twilight after sundown, 23-year-old explorer Etienne Brûlé looked out over Lake Ontario at the mouth of the Humber River, and became the first European to see Lake Ontario. Accompanied by twelve Huron natives, Brûlé had traveled from their village on Lake Simcoe down the 45-km portage route known as the Toronto Carrying-Place Trail along the Humber River Valley to Lake Ontario.

The Toronto Carrying-Place Trail was well-traveled by the natives who gave the name Toronto, which meant "carrying place" or "meeting place," to the area at the mouth of the Humber River. This trail was used by explorers, missionaries and traders until Lieutenant Governor John Simcoe built Yonge Street in 1796. Simcoe named the river after the Humber River in Devonshire, England.

PUBLIC TRANSIT: Take the subway to the Old Mill station (on the Bloor-Danforth line). Exit from the station onto Humber Boulevard and go right.

Turn right again on Old Mill Road. As you walk down the hill, the remains of the Old Mill are on your right. Made of stones quarried from the Humber River Valley, this mill dates from 1848. Sawmills were located here for cutting lumber to build the new settlement of York which became the city of Toronto. Cross the Old Mill Bridge, built in 1916, and descend the stairs on your left to the path along the Humber River.

AUTOMOBILE: From Bloor Street West, turn north onto Humber Boulevard, located several streets west of Jane Street. Go right on Old Mill Road. Cross the Old Mill Bridge and turn left at the entrance to Etienne Brûlé Park. The path is at the parking lot.

THE WALK: The path follows the banks of the Humber River through Etienne Brûlé Park. Here are picnic tables, barbecue pits and washroom facilities. Just before the Dundas Street bridge, a path on the right leads up to Dundas Street from where you can take the Lambton 30 bus east to the High Park subway station or west to the Kipling subway station (both on the Bloor-Danforth line).

North of the Dundas Street footbridge, the path goes through wooded Lambton Park and comes to a long footbridge across the Humber River. On the bridge are benches for you to sit and enjoy the view of the river.

Past the bridge, the path goes under a railway bridge and then through a wooded area, emerging at James Gardens. Here are picnic tables and barbecue pits. On the other side of the Humber River is a golf course and the point where Black

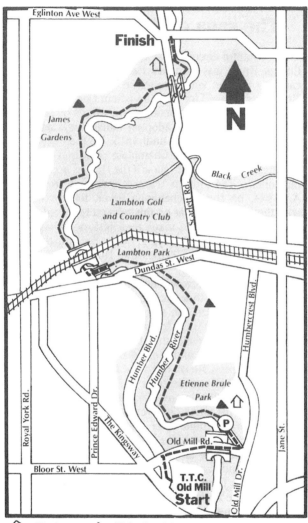

Eglinton Ave West

Finish

N

James Gardens

Black Creek

Scarlett Rd.

Lambton Golf and Country Club

Lambton Park

Dundas St. West

Humber Blvd.

Humber River

Humbercrest Blvd.

Etienne Brule Park

Royal York Rd.

Prince Edward Dr.

The Kingsway

Jane St.

P

Old Mill Rd.

Bloor St. West

Old Mill Dr.

T.T.C. Old Mill Start

⇧ = **Washrooms**   ▲ = **Water Fountain**

Creek flows into the Humber River. A trail sign a bit farther north indicates washrooms are 1/4 km to the left.

Follow the path under the Scarlett Road bridge. The path goes through open parkland to the corner of Eglinton Avenue West and Scarlett Road.

GETTING BACK: You can retrace your route back your starting point. Or, from Eglinton Avenue West, you can cross Scarlett Road and take the Eglinton West 32 bus east to the Eglinton West subway station (on the Spadina line) or the Eglinton subway station (on the Yonge Street line). If you are going back to your car near Old Mill, you can take the Scarlett 79 bus to the Runnymede subway station (on the Bloor-Danforth line) and go west for two stops to Old Mill station.

Etienne Brûlé at the mouth of the Humber River on Lake Ontario from a drawing by C.W. Jeffreys.

14. Humber River and West Humber River

6 km

The Humber River played a key role in the rural economy of the 18th and 19th centuries. The Humber Valley was known for the grist mills and saw mills that were powered by the swift-flowing river. In 1793, Lieutenant Governor John Graves Simcoe introduced a policy to encourage the building of water-driven mills on rivers that were navigable. A number of mills were built on the Humber River, including a sawmill on the river's west bank in this area.

The Humber River flows from its source near Orangeville to Lake Ontario. The West Humber River begins near Caledon. The two branches join near this walking route in northwestern Toronto.

PUBLIC TRANSIT: From Finch subway station (on the Yonge Street line) take the Finch West 36A or 36B bus to Islington Avenue. Or, from Islington subway station (on the Bloor-Danforth line), take the Islington 37C or 37D bus to Finch Avenue West. From Finch Avenue and Islington Avenue, walk north on the west side of Islington Avenue to Rowntree Mills Park, and enter the park.

AUTOMOBILE: The entrance to Rowntree Mills Park is on Islington Avenue, north of Finch Avenue West. Drive along the park road to a parking lot.

THE WALK: At the first parking lot as you enter

Rowntree Mills Park is the trail leading south. Follow this path as it leads under the Finch Avenue West bridge and along the Humber River.

After about 3 km you reach an unsigned trail junction where to the left a path crosses a footbridge with power lines overhead. (This side-trail leads south along the Humber river to Fair Glen Crescent and Weston Road located south of Highway 401.)

To continue this walk, go straight at this junction and stay on the main path. You are now walking along the West Humber River. Cross Albion Road at the traffic lights at Arcot Boulevard on one side of Albion Road and Irwin Road on the other. Follow the trail along the West Humber River to the Islington Avenue bridge.

From here, you can continue walking for about 6 km along the West Humber River Trail to the Humber Arboretum, described separately in this guide.

GETTING BACK: To get back to the walk's start at Rowntree Mills Park, you can also walk north on Islington Avenue or take the Islington 37C or 37D bus to Finch Avenue West.

To get to a subway, you can take the Islington 37C or 37D bus south to Islington subway station (on the Bloor-Danforth line). You can also go north on Islington Avenue to Finch Avenue West and take the Finch West 36 to Finch subway station (on the Yonge Street line). To cross Islington Avenue, the nearest traffic lights are south at Fordwich Crescent.

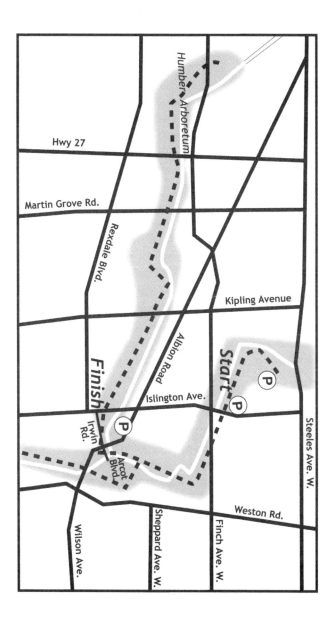

The benefits of walking

"Unhappy businessmen, I am convinced, would increase their happiness more by walking six miles every day than by any conceivable change of philosophy."

—Bertrand Russell

- **Walking is a great social activity**. Share it with family and friends.
- **Walking is inexpensive.** It doesn't require special equipment. All you need is comfortable shoes.
- **When you walk you're immersed in the outdoors.** It lets you get closer to nature. You can enjoy the quiet and hear the birds and the flowing of a stream. You're going slow enough to experience the environment you're walking through.
- **Walking helps you feel energized.** It gives you more stamina and helps breathing and digestion. It also helps your heart and circulation. When you are sedentary, the heart muscle works harder to circulate the blood. When you walk, the legs muscles give the blood an extra push that lessens the load on the heart and helps to lower blood pressure.

15. Humber Arboretum

12 km of interconnecting trails

Situated on 120 hectares in the West Humber River Valley, the Humber Arboretum's self-guided trails go through old forest of maple, beech, ash, oak and hickory, as well as meadows, wetlands and gardens. Wildlife includes frogs, turtles, muskrats, beaver and many species of birds including Great horned owls, heron and kingfisher.

There are also ponds, gazebos and benches. The Nature Orientation Center is an educational facility with displays and exhibits. From here you have a view of the woods, meadows and gardens. Open year round during daylight hours, the Humber Arboretum is managed by the Humber College of Applied Arts and Technology, Toronto and Region Conservation Authority, and City of Toronto. A variety of programs are offered, including nature walks and school programs. For information: telephone (416) 675-5009, www.humberarboretum.on.ca email: nature centre@humber.ca

PUBLIC TRANSIT: From Wilson subway station (on the Spadina line) take the Wilson 96 bus to Humber College Boulevard and entrance "A" to Humber College. From Finch subway station (on the Yonge Street line), take the Finch West 36B bus to Finch Avenue West and Humber College Boulevard. Walk along Humber College Boulevard to entrance "A." From Westwood Mall in Mississauga, you can take Mississauga Transit bus 22 to Humber College Boulevard and entrance "A."

From entrance "A," follow the signs to the Arboretum entrance opposite parking lot number 1. **AUTOMOBILE:** From Highway 27, go west on Humber College Boulevard (located south of Finch Avenue West). Go left into entrance "A" and follow the signs for the Arboretum to parking lot 1. Parking is free. Get a parking pass for the Arboretum at the parking kiosk.

THE WALK: A network of interconnecting trails explore the variety of habitats in the Arboretum. Signs on trees and plants explain their name and origin. Several trails link to the West Humber Trail, a paved walking and bicycling path along the West Humber River.

Among the Arboretum's features is the Woodlot and Meadow Garden, a fringe Carolinian hardwood forest of ash, maple, beech, and ironwood trees. The Dunington Grubb Gardens, near the Nature Centre, are ornamental gardens.

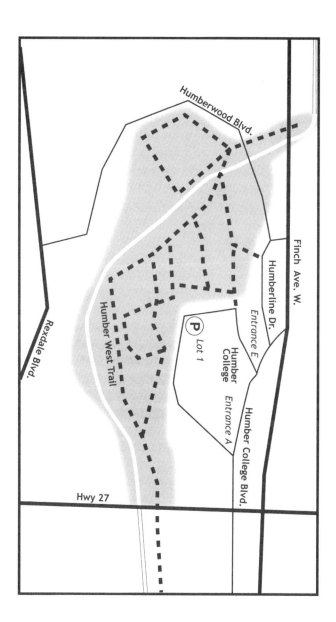

"I have two doctors, my left leg and my right."

— G.M. Trevelyan

16. Taylor Creek

5 km

Though within the 344 square km area drained by the Don River is the highest average density of population in Canada, the wooded valley of Taylor Creek, a major tributary of the Don, is a peaceful respite where over 200 species of birds have been observed. This walk through wooded Taylor Creek valley to the Forks of the Don river can be combined with the Wilket Creek walk for a total of 10 km.

PUBLIC TRANSIT: Take the Bloor-Danforth subway to Victoria Park station and exit onto Victoria Park Avenue. Turn right and walk down Victoria Park Avenue. Cross to the west side of the street at the traffic lights at Crescent Town Road and continue to a sign reading "Sunnybrook Park 10 km, Edwards Gardens 10 km." Turn left here and go down the stairs.

AUTOMOBILE: There are parking lots at both ends of the walk. To reach the end near Victoria Park Avenue, drive along Danforth Avenue and turn north on Dawes Road (several streets west of Victoria Park Road), and take the turn-off for the park just before the bridge over the creek. Begin walking from the parking lot, which is a short distance west of the Victoria Park Road.

To reach the other end of this walk, take the Don Valley Parkway and exit for Don Mills Road North. Keep to the right on the curve of the cloverleaf and take the first exit on the right marked "Taylor Creek Park." Follow the road under the Don Valley Parkway to a parking lot next to the path.

THE WALK: After descending the steps from Victoria Park Road, follow the path. Go under the Dawes Road bridge and cross a footbridge over a small stream to picnic tables, barbecue pits and washroom facilities. Footbridges at several places along the trail permit you to walk the path on either side of the creek.

Before the O'Connor Drive bridge is a path leading up to O'Connor Drive. If you want to end the hike here, you can take the Woodbine 91 bus to Woodbine subway station, or the O'Connor 70 bus to Coxwell subway station (both on the Bloor-Danforth line).

Continuing along the path, you come to public washrooms just before the O'Connor Drive bridge. When you reach a parking lot, you are near the end of Taylor Creek. This area is known as the Forks of the Don as several of the river's tributaries converge here.

Follow the signs left for Sunnybrook Park and Edwards Gardens, and walk across the arched narrow bridge. Climb the hill and cross the footbridge over the railway tracks. After crossing, don't go up the stairs in front of you, but turn left and go along the walkway under Don Mills Road. Walk straight to a sign reading "Edwards Gardens 5 km, Sunnybrook Park 5 km."

From here you can retrace your route back to the walk's start. If you want to continue on the Wilket Creek walk, go right here and follow that

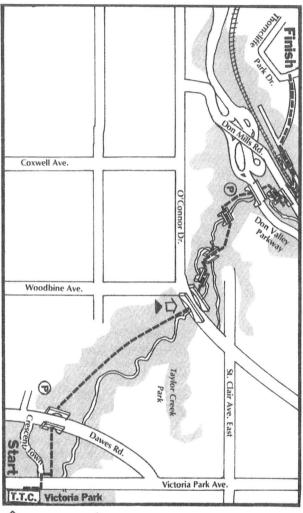

Coxwell Ave.

Woodbine Ave.

O'Connor Dr.

Thorncliffe Park Dr.

Finish

Don Mills Rd.

Don Valley Parkway

Taylor Park

St. Clair Ave. East

Taylor Creek

Dawes Rd.

Crescent Town

Start

Victoria Park Ave.

T.T.C. Victoria Park

⌂ = Washrooms   ▲ = Water Fountain

walk. To take the TTC, turn left here and follow the road parallel to the railway tracks. Then turn right up the hill leading to Thorncliffe Park Drive. A sign here reads: "E.T. Seton Park, Central Don." **GETTING BACK:** To your right on Thorncliffe Park Drive is the Thorncliffe Park 81 bus, which goes to the Pape subway station (on the Bloor-Danforth line). It stops on this side of the street after 3:30 p.m. Before 3:30 p.m. it circles Thorncliffe Park Drive on the other side of the street. If you left your car near the Victoria Park Road end of the walk, take the subway from Pape station east to Victoria Park station.

You can also take the South Leaside 88 bus (no Sunday service) from either side of Thorncliffe Park Drive (take the bus that comes first) to St. Clair subway station (on the Yonge Street line).

17. The Beaches

3 km

One of the most popular walks in Toronto, the picturesque Beaches boardwalk beside sandy beaches on Lake Ontario is often full of walkers, baby carriages and dogs. Though not as wild as the ravines, the Beaches boardwalk offers a beautiful view of Lake Ontario.

During the evenings you can watch the lights of Great Lake freighters blink in the twilight. During a hot summer's day, the Beaches are covered with picnickers and sunbathers. Seagulls and ducks are in abundance.

PUBLIC TRANSIT: There are several ways of reaching the Beaches. You can take the Queen Street East 501 streetcar from Osgoode subway station (on the University line) or Queen subway station (on the Yonge Street line), east to any stop between Coxwell Avenue and Balsam Avenue, and walk south down to the lake.

Three Bloor-Danforth line subway stations also provide access to the Beaches. From Coxwell station, take the Coxwell 22 bus to Queen Street East. From Woodbine station, take the Woodbine South 92 bus to Lake Shore Boulevard East. From Main station, take the Main 64 bus south to Queen Street East. From Queen Street East, it's a short walk south to the Beaches boardwalk and Lake Ontario.

AUTOMOBILE: Take the Lake Shore Boulevard East and turn off at the entrance to Ashbridges

Bay Park and Woodbine Beach (opposite Coxwell Avenue) and follow the signs to the parking lots.
THE WALK: The Beaches boardwalk is accessible from many points. The easternmost part, along a section known as Balmy Beach, begins at Silver Birch Avenue just west of the water filtration plant. This part of the walk is bordered by large oak trees until Wineva Avenue.

West of Wineva Avenue, the boardwalk goes along Kew Gardens which has baseball diamonds. At the base of Woodbine Avenue is the Beaches Olympic Pool. West of the pool, the boardwalk curves around the bay onto Ashbridges Bay Park, a grassy peninsula that juts into Lake Ontario. The boardwalk ends at the tip of the peninsula where there are benches and shelters from sun and rain.

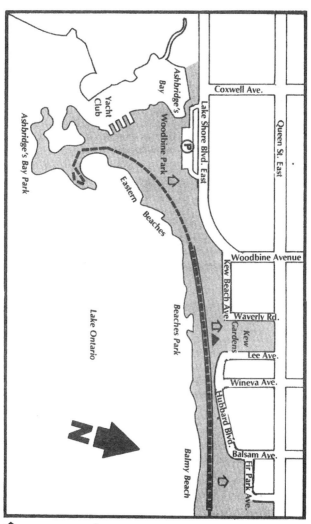

Ashbridge's Bay

Yacht Club

Ashbridge's Bay Park

Coxwell Ave.

Lake Shore Blvd. East

Queen St. East

Woodbine Park

P

Eastern Beaches

Woodbine Avenue

Kew Beach Ave.

Waverly Rd.

Kew Gardens

Lee Ave.

Beaches Park

Lake Ontario

Wineva Ave.

Hubbard Blvd.

Balsam Ave.

N

Balmy Beach

Fir Park Ave.

 - Washrooms   ▲ - Water Fountain

Afoot and light-hearted I take to the open road,
Healthy, free, the world before me,
The long brown path before me leading wherever
I choose.

— Walt Whitman

18. Scarborough Bluffs

4 km of trails

Steep cliffs towering 90 meters over the blue waters of Lake Ontario, the Scarborough Bluffs offer spectacular natural scenery. At the base of the Bluffs is Bluffers Park which juts into Lake Ontario and has walking paths that explore ponds and a driftwood-strewn sand beach.

Carved over thousands of years by the pounding waves of Lake Ontario and eroded by winter frosts and spring rains, the Scarborough Bluffs record five glacial ages, demarcated by the layers of sand that at one time were the floors of pre-historic lakes. The oldest goes back one and a half billion years to the Precambrian Age, the period when the Canadian Shield that covers northern Ontario was formed.

Scarborough was named by Elizabeth Simcoe, wife of Lieutenant Governor John Simcoe. The bluffs here reminded her of the cliffs at the North Sea resort of Scarborough, Yorkshire, England about which the well-known centuries-old British folk-song "Are You Going to Scarborough Fair" was written.

PUBLIC TRANSIT: Go to Warden subway station (on the Bloor Danforth line), and take the Markham 102 or Bellamy 9 bus to the corner of St. Clair Avenue East and Brimley Road. Go right and walk south on Brimley Road. For safety, walk facing traffic. The address on the Bluffers Park sign is 1 Brimley Road South.

AUTOMOBILE: Get on Kingston Road, which is Highway 2, and go south on Brimley Road all the way down to Bluffers Park and the parking lots. The address on the Bluffers Park sign is 1 Brimley Road South.

THE WALK: When you reach the bottom of Brimley Road, there are two areas to explore. You can go right to a network of paths and footbridges over lagoons, ponds and along Lake Ontario. You can see Canada geese, ducks and other waterfowl.

Going left from the bottom of Brimley Road, follow the signs to the beach. From the parking lot, you can explore the sand beach and walk on a path beside the beach. Where the beach ends, you can continue along the base of the bluffs. Explore this wild area and then retrace your route to get back to the start.

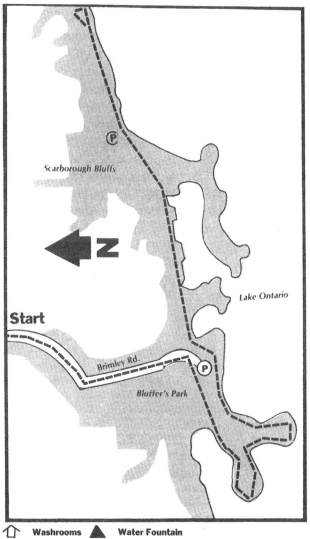

Start

Scarborough Bluffs

Lake Ontario

Brimley Rd.

Bluffer's Park

 Washrooms Water Fountain

More benefits of walking

- **Walking can help you lose weight and keep weight off.** Walking at a moderate pace for 30-60 minutes burns stored fat and can build muscle.
- **Walking helps clear your mind.** When trying to solve a problem, go for a walk and let ideas and solutions come to you. Plato expounded his philosophy while walking in an olive grove.
- **Walking is relaxing.** When you're stressed, angry or feel a painful emotion, the muscles in the body become tense. Walking at a steady pace releases the tension in your muscles and causes the mind to relax.
- **Walking makes you feel good.** Walking increases feel-good endorphins in the brain which can create a sense of euphoria. It can also help lift depression.
- **Walking is good for the brain.** It can make you mentally sharper and may reduce the risk of a decline in thinking abilities and dementia as a person ages.
- **Walking helps you sleep better.** If you're inactive, when you go to bed your mind may be tired but your body isn't. After walking, your body is truly tired and sleep comes easily. Charles Dickens cured his insomnia with nightly walks.

19. Highland Creek

6 km

In the 1830s when this area was settled for farming, 86-tonne schooners navigated almost a kilometer and a half up Highland Creek. Large stands of pine and hardwood trees supplied the saw mills. Trout could be caught in the streams. Although most of the farms are gone and the creek is not as wide and deep as 150 years ago, the walk along Highland Creek, a wide creek flowing through a wooded rural area, retains its rural character.

PUBLIC TRANSIT: Take the subway to the Kennedy station (on the Bloor-Danforth line). From there, take the Scarborough 86 bus to the junction of Kingston Road and Old Kingston Road and walk down Old Kingston Road. Just past the "Welcome to Colonel Danforth Park, Highland Creek" sign is a parking lot. The walk begins here.

AUTOMOBILE: Take Lawrence Avenue East and go northeast on Kingston Road. Go left onto Old Kingston Road and down the hill to the parking lot just after the "Welcome to Colonel Danforth Park, Highland Creek" sign. Park your car here.

THE WALK: From the parking lot, follow the path. Turn left when you reach the main trail along Highland Creek. Cross the footbridge over the creek. You then come to another footbridge and stay on the main path on your side of the creek.

After passing under the Morningside Avenue bridge and crossing a footbridge, you enter

Morningside Park which has picnic tables and washroom facilities.

The trail meanders along the creek. Keep on the trail as it skirts a road and goes back into the woods and descends to the creek and reaches the Lawrence Avenue East bridge.

If you want to end the walk here, you can go up the hill on the left to Lawrence Avenue East and take the Lawrence East 54 bus west to Lawrence East station (on the Scarborough RT line) and Eglinton subway station (on the Yonge Street line).

To continue this walk, stay on the trail to its end at Greenvale Park. The address on the park sign is 10 Greenvale Terrace.

GETTING BACK: From the end of the trail in Greenvale Park, you can retrace your route to the start of the walk. Or, you can go left on Greenvale Terrace to Celeste Drive. Go right on Celeste Drive to Kingston Road. From here you can take the Scarborough 86 bus west to Kennedy subway station (on the Bloor-Danforth line). To get back to the walk's start, cross Kingston Road at the traffic lights and take the Scarborough 86 bus east to Old Kingston Road and walk down Old Kingston Road to this walk's starting point. The Guildwood GO Train station is on the south side of Kingston Road near Celeste Drive. For the GO Transit schedule, go to www.gotransit.ca or telephone 416-869-3200 or toll-free 1-888-GET ON GO (438-6646).

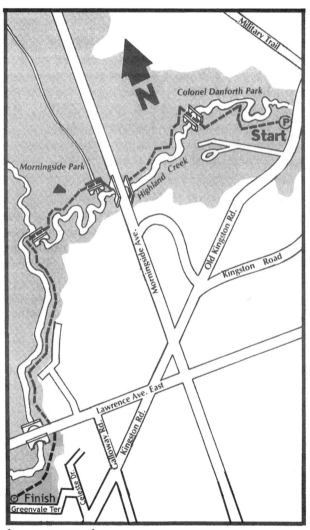

Military Trail

Colonel Danforth Park

N

P
Start

Morningside Park

Highland Creek

Morningside Ave.

Old Kingston Rd.

Kingston Road

Lawrence Ave. East

Galloway Rd.

Kingeston Rd.

Celeste Dr.

 Finish
Greenvale Ter

⌂ = Washrooms   ▲ = Water Fountain

20. Lower Highland Creek and East Point Park

East Point Park 2 km
Lower Highland Creek 2.5 km

East Point Park and Lower Highland Creek offer trails that explore wild parts of the Lake Ontario shoreline. In East Point Park, a path goes through diverse plant life on the edge of the Scarborough Bluffs that rise 33 meters over Lake Ontario.

The Lower Highland Creek path leads along a sand beach covered with driftwood to the mouth of the creek and then up its wooded valley. Along Highland Creek is a mature forest of red oak, eastern hemlock, white pine and sugar maple trees.

PUBLIC TRANSIT: There are several ways to reach these trails.

From Kennedy subway station (on the Bloor-Danforth line), you can:

- Take the Scarborough 86A or 86B bus to Lawrence Avenue East and Beechgrove Drive. From here, walk down Beechgrove Drive to the parking lot for East Point Park. Or, you can start the trail at the southeast corner of Lawrence Avenue East and Beechgrove Drive (walking in the opposite direction than it's described here).

- Take the Scarborough 86D (no Saturday or Sunday service) to Beechgrove Drive and Coronation Drive, and walk east and south on Beechgrove Drive to the parking lot for East Point Park.
- Take the Morningside 116A bus to Morningside Avenue and Coronation Drive. Go right (east) on Coronation Drive to Beechgrove Drive. Continue east and then south on Beechgrove Drive to the parking lot for East Point Park.

From Eglinton subway station (on the Yonge Street line) or Lawrence East RT station (on the Scarborough RT line), take the Lawrence East 54 bus to Lawrence Avenue East and Beechgrove Drive. From here you can walk down Beechgrove Drive to the parking lot for East Point Park. Or, you can also start the trail at the southeast corner of Lawrence Avenue East and Beechgrove Drive (walking in the opposite direction than it's described here).

AUTOMOBILE: From Lawrence Avenue East, go south on Beechgrove Drive (located between Morningside Avenue and Meadowvale Road). Stay on Beechgrove Drive as it turns several times. At the end of the street is the parking lot for East Point Park.

THE WALKS: East Point Park: The trail to East Point Park begins at the parking lot. Follow the wild path along the edge of the bluffs overlooking Lake Ontario. The path eventually emerges in a field behind the F.J. Morgan Water Treatment Plant on Copperfield Road. From here, you can return by the same path or walk out to Copperfield Road, go right on Copperfield Road and walk along the road to the starting point at the East Point Park parking lot.

Lower Highland Creek: From the parking lot for East Point Park, walk out of the parking lot to the Highland Creek Treatment Plant at 51 Beechgrove Drive. When you face the plant, the trail is on the right of the building. Follow the trail as it descends to sand beaches and driftwood on a wild section of the Lake Ontario shoreline. The trail climbs as you approach Highland Creek and the point where the creek flows into Lake Ontario. The trail goes under the railway bridge and then follows Highland Creek.

At the Lawrence Avenue East bridge over Highland Creek, you can retrace your route back to the parking lot at East Point Park, continue following Highland Creek (described separately in this guide), or go left on a side trail to the southeast corner of Lawrence Avenue East and Beechgrove Drive.

GETTING BACK: From Lawrence Avenue East and Beechgrove Drive, you can cross Lawrence Avenue East at the nearest traffic lights and take a Scarborough 86 bus to Kennedy subway station (on the Bloor-Danforth line). You can also take a Lawrence East 54 bus to the Lawrence East RT station (on the Scarborough RT line) or the Eglinton subway station (on the Yonge Street line).

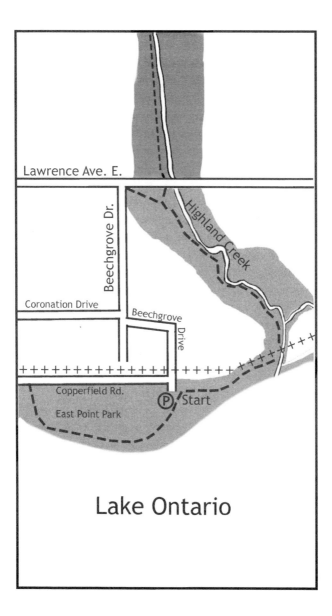

Lawrence Ave. E.

Beechgrove Dr.

Highland Creek

Coronation Drive

Beechgrove Drive

Copperfield Rd.

East Point Park

(P) Start

Lake Ontario

21. Rouge River

4.2 km or 3.1 km loop

Situated near the Toronto Zoo, this route offers rustic country walking. Before the arrival of the Europeans, the Iroquois natives who lived along the Rouge River called it Katabokokonk, meaning river of easy entrance. After the Europeans came, the Rouge River was a portage route for fur traders traveling from Lake Ontario to Lake Simcoe.

Flowing through one of the most wild areas within Toronto, the Rouge River meanders through a wide wooded valley with abundant wildlife. Birds in the Rouge River valley include Common pheasant, Ruffed grouse and American woodcock. Among the animal life is raccoon, red fox, cotton-tail rabbit, European hare, woodchuck, grey squirrel, red squirrel, muskrat, skunk, mink and weasel.

Near the southern end of this route is a campground. From the walk's southern end it's possible, besides taking the TTC bus, to take GO Transit to downtown. Call for the schedule before heading out. See the "Getting Back" section for more details.

PUBLIC TRANSIT: This walk starts at the Pearse House Rouge Valley Conservation Centre, a restored pioneer home, at 1749 Meadowvale Road, just east of the Toronto Zoo. The TTC bus stop for Pearse House is on Meadowvale Road near the overpass for the zoo. To get here from

Kennedy subway station (on the Bloor Danforth line), take the Scarborough 86A bus which operates every day during the summer, and Monday to Friday during the rest of the year.

From Sheppard-Yonge subway station or Don Mills subway station (on the Sheppard line), on weekends and holidays take the Sheppard East 85A or 85B to Pearse House; on weekdays take the Sheppard East 85 bus to Sheppard Avenue East and Meadowvale Road, and then take the Scarborough 86A bus north to Pearse House.

AUTOMOBILE: To reach Pearse House, take Highway 401 east and exit onto Meadowvale Road. Follow the signs north toward the Toronto Zoo and take the exit ramp for the zoo. At the top of the ramp, turn right to Pearse House. There is parking here.

Near the route's mid-point there is parking on Twyn Rivers Drive. To get there, go east on Sheppard Avenue East. Just past Meadowvale Road, take Twyn Rivers Drive —which is on the left as Sheppard Avenue East goes to the right. Descend into the valley to the parking lot.

At the southern end of the walk, there is parking at Glen Rouge Park. Enter at the sign reading "Glen Rouge Park, Rouge River" on Kingston Road-Highway 2 east of Sheppard Avenue East.

THE WALK: From the Pearse House parking lot, take the 1.5 km Vista Trail. Follow the trail as it passes under power lines and then goes along a ridge with scenic views in both directions. The trail gradually descends to Twyn Rivers Drive.

From here you can take the Orchard Trail back to Pearse House, or continue south on the Riverside Trail to Highway 2.

To the Orchard Trail: Go left on Twyn Rivers Drive, cross the bridge over the Little Rouge River to the sharp turn in the road. The Orchard Trail begins between the two stone posts. A trail map is posted at the entrance. The trail leads through a wooded area to the valley edge overlooking the Little Rouge River. The trail gradually descends to the river, crosses under power lines and then climbs to a flat area and a road. Go left on the road to Pearse House.

To the Riverside Trail: Cross Twyn Rivers Drive and go right. At the first sharp turn in the road is the start of the trail. The trail traverses sandy riverbank, forests and meadows. Just before the Kingston Road-Highway 2 bridge, cross a footbridge over the Rouge River. Follow the path up to the parking lot. Walk past Glen Rouge Camping to Kingston Road-Highway 2.

GETTING BACK: Turn right on Kingston Road-Highway 2 and walk to the intersection of Sheppard Avenue East. From here, there are several ways to get back to central Toronto.

You can go right on Sheppard Avenue and take the Sheppard East 85A bus to Don Mills subway station (on the Sheppard line) and Sheppard-Yonge subway station. To get back to the walk's start, take the Sheppard East 85A bus on weekends and holidays to Pearse House, or on weekdays take the Sheppard East 85A to Sheppard Avenue East and Meadowvale Road

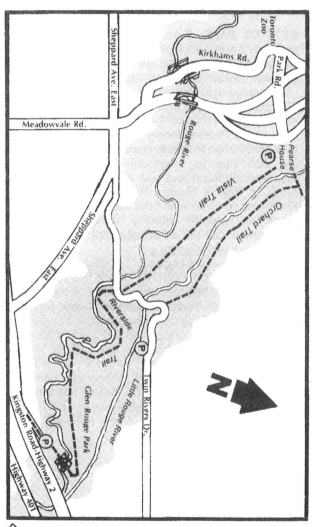

 – Washrooms ▲ – Water Fountain

and then take the Scarborough 86A north to
Pearse House. From Meadowvale Road and
Sheppard Avenue you can also take the
Scarborough 86 bus to Kennedy subway station
(on the Bloor-Danforth line).

On Kingston Road-Highway 2 at Sheppard
Avenue East is a GO Transit bus stop (called the
"North Rouge – Kingston Road at Port Union
Road" bus stop on the GO schedule). GO buses
that stop here go to GO bus stations at York Mills
subway station (on the Yonge Street line) and
Yorkdale subway station (on the Spadina subway
line). It's also possible to take the GO train from
the Rouge Hill GO train station to Union Station
(at the southern end of both north-south subway
lines). To get to the Rouge Hill GO train station,
cross Sheppard Avenue and take the Sheppard
East 85A bus. For GO Transit schedules go to
www.gotransit.ca or telephone (416) 869-3200, or
toll-free 1-888-GET ON GO (438-6646).

22. Rouge Beach

2 km

Rouge Beach is a sand beach where the Rouge River flows into Lake Ontario. Here was the Seneca native village called Ganatsekwyagon, meaning "among the birches." Red clay in the river's banks give the water a distinct colour. French explorers in the 18th century called the waterway Riviere Rouge.

On the way to Rouge Beach, you pass the Rouge Marshes that are a stopover point for migratory birds. Waterfowl breed here. In the marshes are channels remaining from a 1920s plan by Cecil White to make this area the "Venice of North America" with bridges and canals like those in Venice. He dredged channels and built a bridge, but the project failed after the 1929 stock market crash. In 1954, Hurricane Hazel's flood waters washed away the remaining bridge structures.

PUBLIC TRANSIT: From Eglinton subway station (on the Yonge Street line) or from Lawrence East RT station (on the Scarborough RT), take the Lawrence East 54 bus to its terminus at Lawrence Avenue East and Starspray Boulevard.

You can also take the GO Train to Rouge Hill near Lawrence Avenue East just east of Port Union. For schedules, go to **www.gotransit.ca** or call (416) 869-3200, or toll-free 1-888-GET ON GO (438-6646).

From the TTC bus stop or the GO Train station, walk east on Lawrence Avenue East to Rouge Hills Drive and the park entrance. The address on the Rouge Beach Park sign is 195 Rouge Hills Drive. After the entering the park you pass the Rouge Marshes and a parking area.

AUTOMOBILE: Go east all the way on Lawrence Avenue East to Rouge Hills Drive, east of Port Union Road. The address on the Rouge Beach Park sign is 195 Rouge Hills Drive. After entering the park, you pass the Rouge Marshes and reach a parking area.

THE WALK: From the end of the parking area, go right and walk under the railway bridge. (The metal footbridge leads to the Waterfront Trail in Pickering, not to Rouge Beach.)

After going under the railway bridge, you're at Rouge Beach and the point where the Rouge River flows into Lake Ontario. Explore the sand beach. Return by the same route.